Jazz Piano Vocabulary

Volume 3
The Phrygian Scale

by Roberta Piket

With additional material available
on-line at www.muse-eek.com

Muse Eek Publishing Company
New York, New York

Copyright © 2004 by Roberta Piket. All rights reserved

ISBN 1594899541

No part of this publication may be reproduced, stored in a
retrieval system, or transmitted, in any form or by any means,
electronic, mechanical, photocopying, recording, or otherwise,
without the prior written permission of the publisher.

Printed in the United States

This publication can be purchased from your local bookstore or by contacting:
Muse Eek Publishing Company
P.O. Box 509
New York, NY 10276, USA
Phone: 212-473-7030
Fax: 212-473-4601
http://www.muse-eek.com
sales@muse-eek.com

Table Of Contents

Acknowledgements	iv
About the Author	v
Foreword	vi
How to Use This Book	vii
Swung Eighth Notes	viii
Order Of Presentation	viii
Fingering	viii
Introduction To The Phrygian Mode	9
Applying The Phrygian Mode To Improvisation	10
Sus♭9 Chord (The "Phrygian Chord")	10
Major triad over major 7th in the bass	13
Using the Phrygian scale over minor 7th chords	15
The Spanish Phrygian Scale	16
Explanation of Left Hand Chord Voicings	19
Phrygian Modes: Fingerings And Left Hand Chord Voicings	21
Hand Position	21
Practice Method	21
Dynamics	22
Using The Left Hand Chord Voicings	22
Swung Eighth Notes, Articulation and Phrasing	22
The Modes	23
A Modal Approach To Chord Voicings And Comping	26
Sample Comping Patterns	29
Your Ideas	32
A Phrygian Etude: Apple Flambe (by Virginia Mayhew)	36
Further Exploration	40

Acknowledgments

The author gratefully acknowledges Bruce Arnold for his invaluable feedback and Muse Eek Publishing for the opportunity to publish this book.

The author would also like to thank Virginia Mayhew for permission to use her composition, *Apple Flambe*, and Mike Garson for permission to use his beautiful artwork.

Special thanks to Billy Mintz for his support and understanding.

About the Author

Roberta Piket is from Queens, NY. Her father, composer Frederick Piket, gave her her first piano lessons when she was seven years old. Roberta began playing seriously in her early teens, studying jazz piano with Walter Bishop, Jr and classical piano with Vera Wels. After graduating from prestigious Hunter College High School, she entered the joint double-degree program at Tufts University and the New England Conservatory of Music, earning a Bachelor's Degree in Computer Science from the former and a Bachelor's Degree in Jazz Studies from the latter. During this time she studied privately with Fred Hersch, Stanley Cowell, Jim McNeely and Bob Moses. Soon after graduation Roberta returned to New York City to devote herself to music full-time, which she has done ever since. In New York, she studied for six years with Richie Beirach and also studied briefly with Sofia Rosoff.

Roberta has performed professionally as a sidewoman with David Liebman, Rufus Reid, Michael Formanek, Lionel Hampton, Mickey Roker, Harvey Wainapel, Eliot Zigmund, Billy Mintz, and the BMI/New York Jazz Orchestra, and has twice been a featured guest on *Marian McPartland's Piano Jazz*, on National Public Radio.

Roberta has taught at Long Island University and has several private students at the Berkeley-Carroll School in Brooklyn. She has also held master classes and/or clinics at the Eastman School of Music, California Institute of the Arts, Rutgers University, Duke University, as well as many other institutions in the U.S., Europe, and Japan.

Roberta has six CDs as a leader which have frequently made the jazz magazines' yearly top ten lists. She currently leads two bands: The *Roberta Piket Trio* and *Alternating Current*. *Piano & Keyboard* recently called Roberta "one of the most accomplished and inventive young jazz pianists currently working on the scene."

More information about Roberta's music can be found at her web sites: www.RobertaJazz.com and www.AlternatingCurrent.info.

Foreword

Many instrumentalists wish to pursue jazz improvisation, but are intimidated because they don't know what notes to play over chord changes, beyond the chord tones themselves. Frequently students who do know what scales they need to learn in order to play over changes are unable to internalize this information to the point of being able to use the scales in an actual playing situation. They may have difficulty learning the notes because they are unsure of what fingerings to use, or they may not have had enough guidance in making the transition from *playing* the scales to *applying* them in a musical situation.

This book explores the Phrygian mode and its use in jazz improvisation. The Phrygian is sometimes considered a more advanced mode because it is used with more complex chord structures that do not appear naturally in the diatonic scales, such as the sus♭9 chord. Before you begin this book, if you are new to improvisation, you may wish to work with one of the following books in this series: Volume 1 (the Major scale); Volume 2 (the Dorian mode) or Volume 5 (the Mixolydian mode). If you are already fluent with using those scales to improvise, then you are ready for this book. In this volume, you will learn to use the Phrygian mode to create voicings and lines that transcend the Be-bop language that we have discussed in those other books. Like the other books in this series, this book offers a workbook to jazz improvisation with melodic examples that you can practice. You can listen to these examples on the Muse Eek website as well. The goal is to provide you with enough guidance to work confidently on your own so that you become comfortable integrating the use of the scales into your improvisation.

This book is part of a series (available as e-books or in paper format) that will focus on learning and applying jazz scales in order to give you the vocabulary and skill to become a fluid jazz improvisor.

Muse Eek Publishing has created a website with a FAQ forum for this book. If you get stuck, or have questions or feedback, please contact me at Roberta@muse-eek.com and I will be happy to respond in the forum.

Roberta Piket
Brooklyn, New York

How To Use This Book

The material in this section has already been presented in previous volumes of the *Jazz Piano Vocabulary* series. If you have studied any of those books you may wish to skip this section. You may find it useful to review, however, in order to brush up on your practice habits.

This series of books assumes that you know how to read music and that you have a basic understanding of the diatonic (major/minor) system. As I mentioned in the foreword, if you are still struggling with these issues you may wish to begin with a different volume. If you need to brush up on your note-reading or diatonic scales, there is an extensive primer in *Jazz Piano Vocabulary: Volume 1 - The Major Scale* on note-reading, intervals, triads, seventh chords and rhythmic notation. If you find anything in this book confusing, please visit the Muse Eek web site at www.muse-eek.com first and check the FAQ section for this book to see if your question has already been answered. If not, use the form on the website to e-mail your questions.

The purpose of this book is to help you learn to improvise using the Phrygian mode. Memorize the scales and fingerings and practice the examples repeatedly until you have mastered them. Execute each example at the piano slowly and carefully to begin. Increase your tempo gradually as your ability increases. Make sure you use the exact same fingerings every time so that you can learn the scales more efficiently as your hand builds muscle memory.

You may wish to use a metronome to be certain that you are not slowing down on difficult passages. Try putting the metronome on the "two and four"; that is, the second and fourth beats of each measure. This emphasis on the "weak" beats instead of the "strong" first and third beats is part of what gives jazz its unique rhythmic character. If it is too difficult for you to play with the metronome on two and four, then first learn the scales with the metronome on the quarter note and then, after you are comfortable with the notes, try the "two and four" again. Eventually it will get easier to feel the music this way and your sense of rhythm will become stronger and more sophisticated.

Play through each exercise smoothly and evenly. As you master each exercise you should gradually increase the tempo while still maintaining complete control. This will help you to develop good habits which will remain with you when you start playing more technically challenging music.

This book contains a great deal of material. You will not be able to learn everything in the book in one sitting. Depending on how fluent you are with scales in general, it may take you anywhere from a few weeks to several months or more to truly master the material in this book. Spend as much time as you need on each item until you have truly mastered it.

Consistency is critical. Even if you have less time on some days than on other days, it is extremely important that you refresh your memory almost every day until the material is completely absorbed. If you do this, you will find that you will progress much more steadily and will save yourself a great deal of frustration.

In the same vein, it is also a good idea to go back to previous material even while moving forward through the book. This will help reinforce what you've already learned, enabling you to build on it. For example, if you have learned the first six Phrygian scales and are working on the seventh, you may want to play through the first six at least once a day until they become second nature so that you don't forget them.

Swung Eighth Notes

As in the previous volumes in this series, each scale is presented in an eighth note pattern (resolving to a quarter note at the last note) to allow for an even four-bar phrase as the scale ascends and descends. By now you should be comfortable playing each exercise with *swung eighth notes*. Recall from previous volumes that in swung (or "swinging") eighth notes, the first eighth note in a pair of eight notes is held twice as long as the second eighth note, giving the notes a relaxed triplet feel.

Order of Presentation

The scales are ordered by key using the *circle of fifths*. The circle of fifths allows us to progress through all the keys by moving either up or down in perfect fifths from one key to the next.

In the scales section of this book we will progress down in fifths, from E Phrygian to A Phrygian to D Phrygian, etc., until we arrive at the last scale, B Phrygian.

Fingering

It is important to use the correct fingering when learning the scales. If you are inconsistent in your fingering you will find it difficult to build muscle memory which will make it more difficult to internalize the material.

Recall that the thumb of each hand is always "1", and the pinky is always "5". If you can remember this then you will quickly become proficient at applying the correct fingerings as you learn to play a passage of written music.

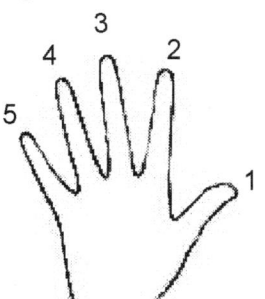 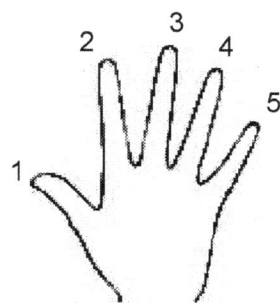

Particularly if you are self-taught, some of these fingerings may at first seem awkward. Give yourself a chance to get used to them. After learning them, if something still feels awkward, you can change it. Everyone's hand is different. However, don't assume they don't work if they feel "funny" the first time you try them. Practice them slowly, making sure to apply them accurately and consistently. Only by applying the correct fingerings every time you play will using them become automatic. Eventually, with enough experience, you will be able to determine the correct fingering on your own.

Introduction To The Phrygian Mode

The modes that developed in Europe during the Medieval period are sometimes known as the "Church modes" because they evolved through the use of Gregorian chant, the sacred monophonic music of Europe's Catholic Church during this period. The Church modes are derived from the Major scale. Each mode has the same notes as the Major scale, but each mode starts and ends on a different note from the Major scale. The seven modes that we use in jazz are: Ionian, Dorian, Phrygian, Lydian, Mixolydian, Aeolian, and Locrian.

This book is concerned with the Phrygian mode. The Phrygian mode is one of several important elements that took jazz out of the Be-bop era and into the sixties with composer/players such as Wayne Shorter, John Coltrane, Joe Henderson, McCoy Tyner and Herbie Hancock. In this book we will learn how to play and apply this mode to unlock a more modern sound in your jazz playing.

The Phrygian mode can be derived by starting and ending on the third note of a Major scale. For example, E is the third note of the C Major scale. Therefore, the E Phrygian mode starts and ends on E and contains all the notes of the C major scale:

E phrygian Mode

Because the E Phrygian mode uses the notes of the C Major scale, C Major is referred to as the *parent scale* of E Phrygian. By knowing the parent scale of a mode, it is easy to figure out the notes that belong to that mode. As another example, if we want play a G Phrygian mode, we would first want to understand that G is the third degree of the E♭ Major scale, makincxg E♭ Major the parent scale of G Phrygian. Thus, the G Phrygian mode starts and ends on G and contains all the notes are found in the E♭ Major scale:

G Phrygian Mode

Understanding the relationship of the Phrygian mode to its parent scale will help you understand the mode's use and will make it easier to learn the notes of each mode. However, this is merely an intermediate step. The goal is to hear and relate to the E Phrygian mode *as* an E Phrygian mode, *not* as a C major scale starting on E. If you do not learn to think and hear beyond the parent scale when using the modes, you are adding an extra step which will interfere with your ability to hear and react instantaneously to whatever chord you encounter when improvising. (If you have trouble hearing the modes and chords and how they relate to each other you may find it helpful to investigate one or more of the ear-training books on the Muse-Eek website.)

Another way to think of the Phrygian mode is in terms of its sequence of whole steps and half steps. The pattern for any Phrygian mode is of course always the same:

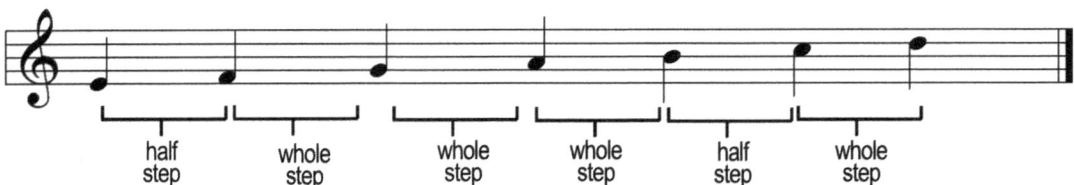

You may notice that this pattern is the same as that of a natural minor scale with the second degree lowered by a half step. For many musicians keeping this in mind is the easiest way to derive the Phrygian modes, at least until you know them by memory.

Choose whatever way of thinking about the Phrygian mode works best for you. Once you learn all the modes and have them under your fingers you will not need to think about them in order to play them

Applying The Phrygian Mode To Improvisation

There are three chords which are commonly derived from the Phrygian mode. We will discuss each of these below.

Sus♭9 Chord (The "Phrygian Chord")

The Phrygian scale is used most commonly over a chord known by at least three different names. It is most frequently called the *sus♭9* chord (for example, Esus♭9). However, another name for the same chord is simply the *Phrygian chord*. If you look at this chord from the bass up, it consists of (after the bass note) the second, fourth, fifth and first notes of the Phrygian scale. Played with the root in the bass, this sound creates a great deal of tension.:

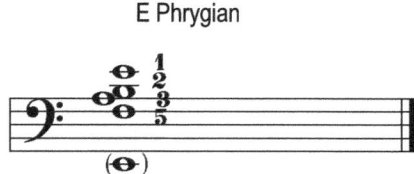

The third name you may see for an E Phrygian chord is Fmaj7♭5/E. This is because, if you look at the notes above the bass note, they form a major 7th♭5 chord with its root a half step above the bass note:

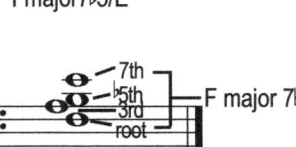

Recall how, in Volume 5 (*The Mixolydian Mode*), we used the sus chord as a substitute for a V chord with the same root, or as a substitute for a ii-V progression, resolving it down a fifth to the tonic. (For example, we substituted Esus or E7sus for E7.) We can use the Phrygian chord in the same way as a substitute for the V or ii-V. So, instead of:

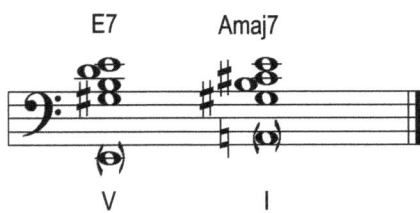

we can use:

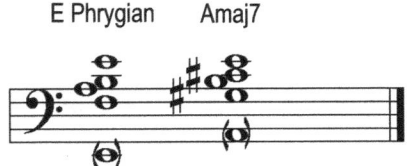

You should practice the above resolution in all keys until using this substitution becomes second nature. Below, space is provided. Write out the notes for the V Phrygian to I Major 7th progression in all twelve keys and learn it. (The voicing for the Phrygian chord in each key is provided with the scales.)

Below another resolution possibility for the Phrygian chord is illustrated. In this progression, we resolve all but the bass note down a half step, so that the bass note becomes the root of the new major seventh chord:

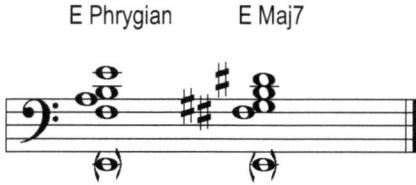

Below space is provided to write the notes for this resolution (I Phrygian to I Major 7th) below in all twelve keys and learn it.

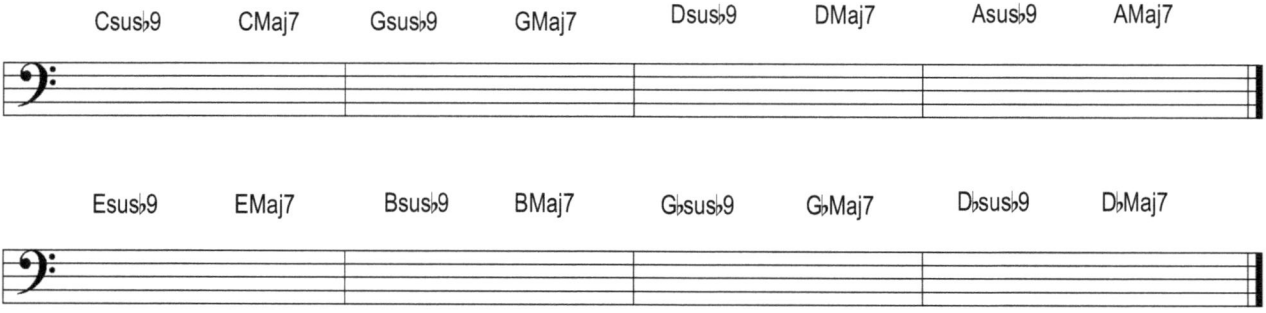

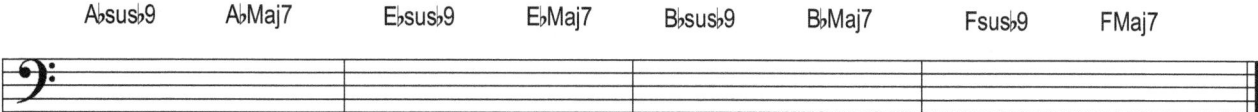

Major triad over major 7th in the bass

The second chord derived from the Phrygian mode is a slash chord consisting of a major triad a half step above the bass note. For example, F/E (F triad over E in the bass) is derived from the E Phrygian scale. If you saw the chord A♭/G (A♭ triad over G in the bass), you would apply the G Phrygian scale. (Since the bass note is the major seventh, this chord can be interpreted as a major triad with its seventh in the bass.)

The major triad/major seventh chord, being closely related to the Phrygian chord, resolves in similar ways. As with the Phrygian chord, you can resolve all but the bass note down a half step, so that the bass note becomes the root of the new major seventh chord:

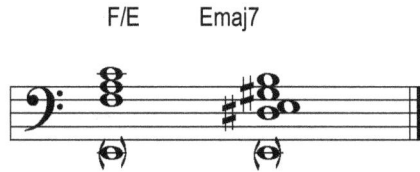

The voicing for this chord in each key is provided with the scales. Note that the voicings shown represent just one possibility. Experiment with inverting the notes to create new voicings.

Write out and practice this progression in all twelve keys the same way you did the progressions using the Phrygian chord. After you learn them, experiment with varying the inversions and tensions.

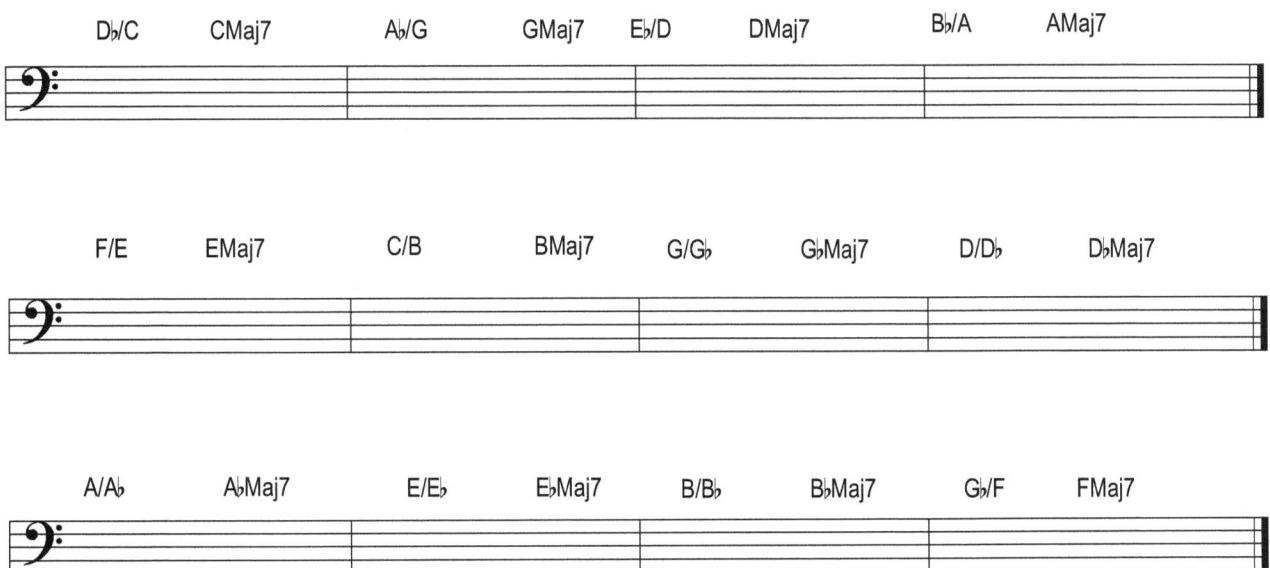

Another resolution using this chord is possible when the chord is treated as a substitute for a V chord or a ii-V progression, the same way we treated the sus♭9 chord above:

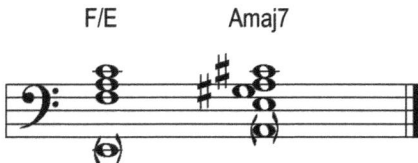

An example of this substitution can be found on Joe Henderson's version of "Night And Day" (*Inner Urge*, Blue Note Records). On the original leadsheet, in the key of D major, first chord of the chorus is B♭maj7, which resolves down a half step to the V chord, A major, and finally from the V to the I chord of D major:

In Joe's version, the first two chords are replaced with B♭/A, which resolves to Dmaj7:

Once again, write out and practice the progression in all twelve keys. Experiment with changing the voicing.

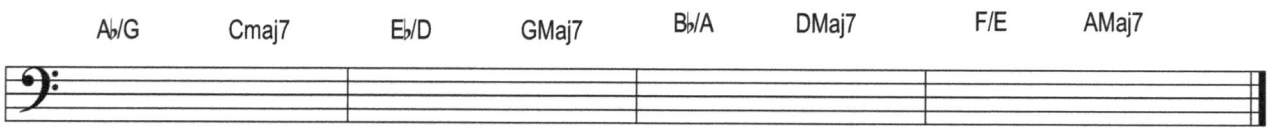

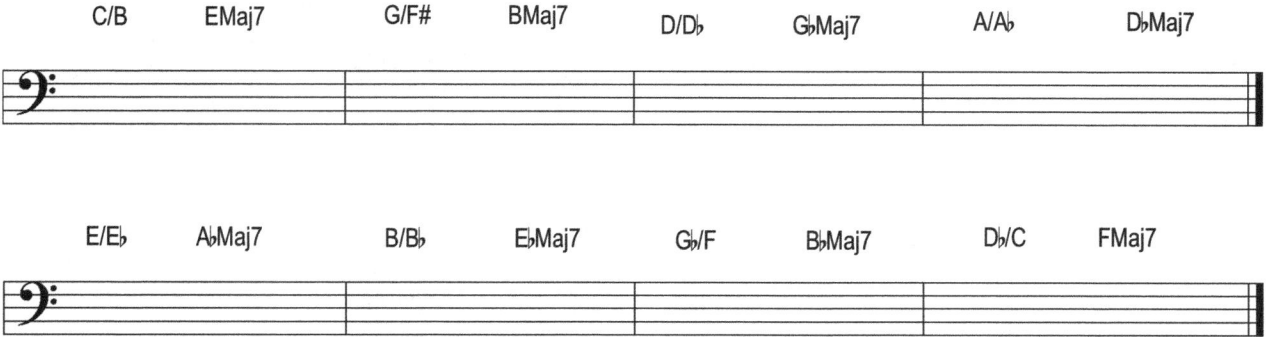

Using the Phrygian scale over minor 7th chords

The Phrygian mode can be used instead of the Dorian mode when improvising over a minor seventh chord. However, it must be used with caution. As you can see below, the E Phrygian mode contains the ♭9 and ♭13 instead of the natural 9 and natural 13 of the Dorian mode. For this reason, the Phrygian scale will not work with left-hand voicings which contain the natural 9th or 13th:

In mainstream Be-Bop jazz, it is best to avoid using the Phrygian mode over a minor seventh chord which functions as the ii chord in the key. For example, in the key of D, if you had the following progression, the best choice in a Be-Bop context would be E Dorian over the E-7 chord. (The scale indicated for each chord is given below each measure.):

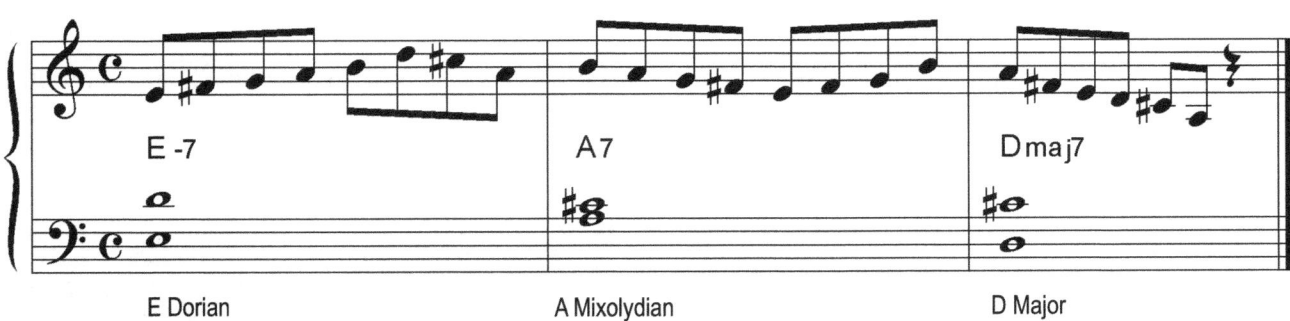

However, if the minor seven chord has a function other than that of the ii chord, you may find that the Phrygian scale sounds good as an alternative or in addition to the Dorian scale. For example, in a iii-VI-ii-V-I progression, the Phrygian scale could be used over the iii chord:

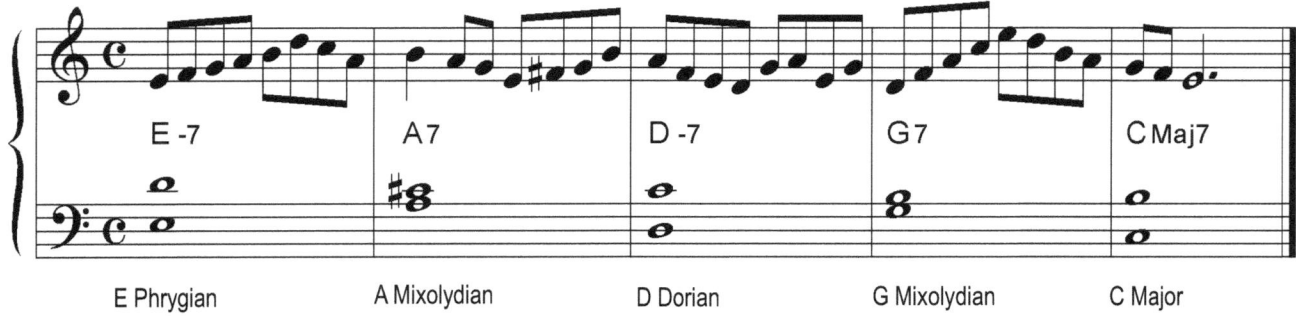

Because the Phrygian scale is not often used over the minor seventh chord, the left hand voicing for the minor seventh chord has not been included with the scales. In the example above we used simple shell voicings (root and seventh or root and third), but any voicing which does not include the ninth or 13th will work.

The Spanish Phrygian Scale

There is a variant of the Phrygian scale of which you should be aware. If you raise the third note of the Phrygian scale a half step you get what is known as the Spanish Phrygian scale. It is also known as the "Phrygian raised 3" or "Phrygian sharp 3" scale:

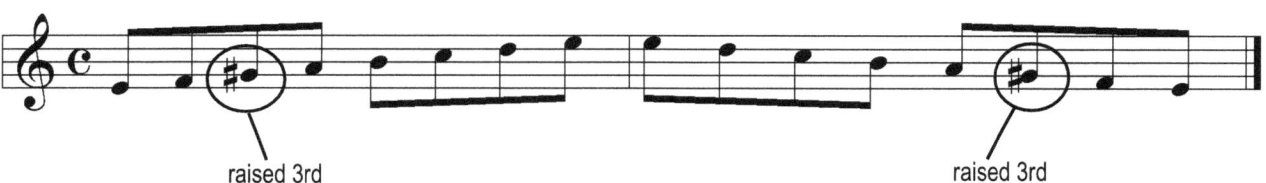

(Note that the parent scale of the Spanish Phrygian scale is the harmonic minor scale a fifth below. For example, the parent scale of D Spanish Phrygian is G harmonic minor.)

The Spanish Phrygian mode can be related to three chords. Two of them are the same as the original Phrygian scale, as we will see below.

The Spanish Phrygian mode can be used over the Phrygian (sus♭9) chord, as you will hear if you play the following example:

I utilized the Phrygian #3 scale over a Phrygian chord in my reharmonization of Jerome Kern's classic, *The Song Is You*. (*Roberta Piket Trio*, <u>Midnight In Manhattan</u>, Meldac Records, 2000). The original bridge begins with a simple cadence in E major:

In my trio version, I replaced the second and third chords with E7sus♭9, or E Phrygian. The G# in the melody implies the Spanish Phrygian mode:

The Spanish Phrygian scale can also be used with the major triad/major 7th chord:

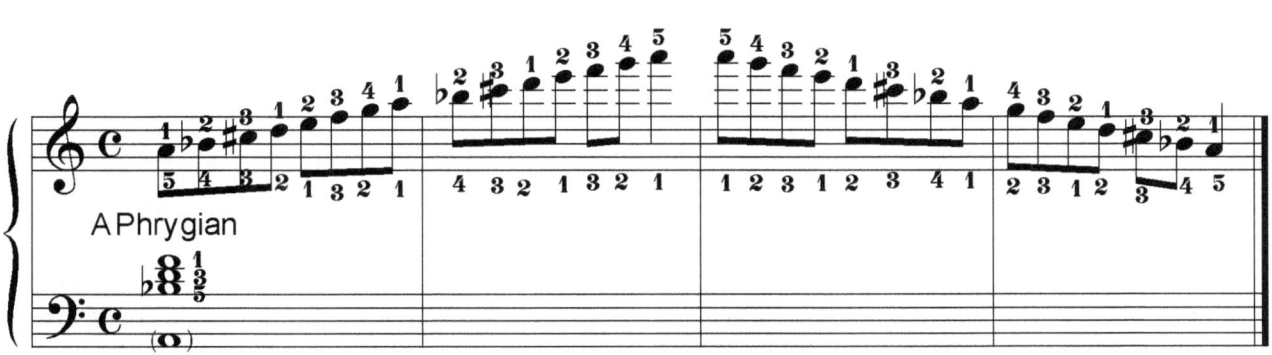

The Spanish Phrygian scale will not work with a minor seventh chord because of the raised (major) third. However, the raised third makes it appropriate to play over a dominant seventh chord:

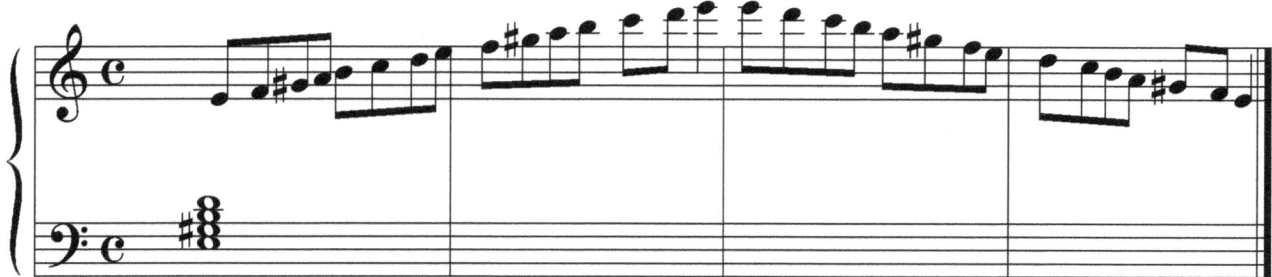

(Note that the regular Phrygian scale will *not* work over a dominant 7th chord because of the scale's lowered third.)

As you can see above, playing the Spanish Phrygian scale over a dominant 7th chord gives us the following tensions: ♭9, 11 and ♭13th.

Sometimes a composer will indicate the Spanish Phrygian scale is intended by using this chord notation: *Phrygian #3* ("Phrygian sharp 3"). This implies the use of the Spanish Phrygian scale over the Phrygian chord. Occasionally you may see "*Spanish Phrygian*" indicated as the chord, but this is unusual.

Because so many of the exact same voicings work for both the Phrygian and the Spanish Phrygian scales, when a Phrygian chord is indicated, it can sometimes be hard to know whether the composer intended the sound of the Phrygian scale or of the Spanish Phrygian scale, assuming the composer is not there to ask,

The following general guidelines may be helpful:

If the composer notates a sus♭9 chord, the chances are that she is thinking of the Spanish Phrygian, since a sus chord generally can contain a major third but not a minor third.

If the composer notates the chord as a Spanish Phrygian chord or, more commonly, a Phrygian #3 chord, he is probably thinking of the Spanish Phrygian scale.

If the chord notated is a major triad/major 7th, the composer may or may not be thinking specifically of one form of the Phrygian scale or the other. In an ambiguous case such as this, you must use your ear and your discretion to obtain greater insight. Start by observing whether the melody uses the minor 3rd of the Phrygian scale or the raised third of the Spanish Phrygian. The piece may use both interchangeably, which gives you some flexibility as to which scale to use. (For an example of this see the etude found later in this book.) You should also pay attention to the other band members' parts. For example, do you hear a specific type of third in the the bass part or horn part?

Finally, I'd like to point out that sometimes when a composer tells you to play a Phrygian chord, she may not have a preference as to whether to use the Phrygian or Spanish Phrygian scale. Frequently the sounds of these scales are used interchangeably.

Keep in mind that when you are soloing, the two scales become more interchangeable and you can mix and match at your discretion. To become as fluent with the Spanish Phrygian as the Phrygian, practice the Spanish Phrygian scale the same way you do the Phrygian scale. You can use the same fingerings as you do for the Phrygian scales. Just remember to sharp the third degree of the scale.

Explanation Of Left Hand Chord Voicings

Once you are comfortable playing the modes in your right hand, the next step is to learn the corresponding chords in the left hand. Eventually you will play these left-hand voicings while playing the mode in the right hand.

Two left-hand chord voicings are provided for you to accompany yourself while playing the corresponding mode in the right hand. One is the sus♭9 chord and the other is the major triad/maj7th chord.

In the first scale, E Phrygian, the E Phrygian chord voicing provided looks like this:

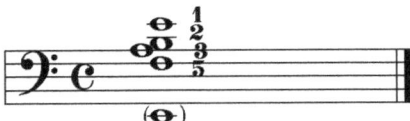

The bass note in parentheses in this chord is not meant to be played in a performance situation. It is only provided so that you can hear the chord against its root when practicing. This type of "rootless" voicing is useful to learn because, when you are playing with a bass player in a real-world situation, it is not always necessary to play each chord's root. The bass player will do that for you (usually).

The second chord illustrated with the E Phrygian scale is the major triad/major 7th chord:

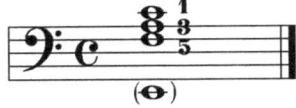

Again, it is useful to hear the bass note but it is not necessary to play it. It is also possible to play this voicing with the bass note a half step below the triad, even if a bass player is doubling it an octave or two below:

The half step in this voicing increases the tension. It is recommended that you try the voicing both ways; that is, as written in the scales section and also with the bass note a half step below the triad. You will find that different variations are approprate in different musical contexts.

Phrygian Modes: Fingerings And Left Hand Chord Voicings

Before you get started learning the scales in all keys, here are a few suggestions and guidelines to help you get the most out of your practice time. If you have read these suggestions in other volumes of this series you can skip this section and go right to the scales.

Hand Position

It is important to develop good habits with respect to hand position. It may not seem important when playing slowly, but when you begin to execute faster passages, you will find that good hand and wrist position will make a difference in your control, thus effecting your ability to play evenly and cleanly.

When playing notes that are close together, as is the case with scales, fingers should be bent, so that you are playing with the balls of your fingers. (If you have long finger nails you will need to cut them to achieve this.) All fingers should be kept in this rounded position whether you are using them or not. (See the picture below.) Of course if you are playing a widely spread chord, your fingers will not be as bent as they are when playing a scale in which each note is adjacent to the next note to be played. The idea is to keep your fingers in a gently bent yet relaxed position.

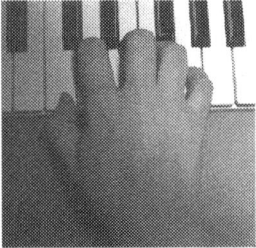

Many inexperienced pianists veer their wrists from side to side, particularly when changing hand position as they go up and down the keyboard while playing a scale. In medical circles this is known as ulnar deviation and is a great way to develop wrist tendonitis (a bad thing). When changing hand position as you ascend or descend the keyboard, do NOT change your wrist position relative to your hand. Instead, as your arm glides up (or down) the keyboard, bring your thumb under you hand and reach for the note. Let your thumb do the stretching, not your wrist. Keep your elbows close to your side.

Practice Method

To begin, practice each scale in the right hand, up two octaves and down two octaves, paying attention to the fingering provided. (Right hand fingering is notated above each note of the scale.) You may find it useful to say each note out loud as you play. Even better for your ear is to try to sing the notes of each scale while playing.

The reason why you should initially focus on learning each scale in your right hand is that once you learn the notes you will be accompanying yourself with the appropriate chord in your left hand, much as your left hand would "comp" while your right hand solos. As a matter of good training and technique, however, it is valuable to master all the Phrygian modes with both hands. For this purpose, left hand fingerings for each Phrygian mode are provided (below each note).

Dynamics

Keep in mind that the left hand is *accompanying* the right hand. Therefore, the left hand should be a bit softer in volume than the right hand. At first it may seem difficult to coordinate your hands in this way, but if you try to *hear* the right hand melody louder, as opposed to merely trying to play harder with your right hand, then eventually you will naturally begin to emphasize the melody more.

Using The Left Hand Chord Voicings

Once you are comfortable playing the scales in your right hand, the next step is to play the corresponding voicing in the left hand while playing the scale in the right hand. As discussed in the previous section, it is suggested that you practice all twelve of the Phrygian modes against the Phrygian chord; then practice all the Phrygian modes again against the major triad/major 7th chord.

The bass note in parentheses below the chord indicates the root of the chord. While you would not play this note in an actual playing situation, it is useful to hear the root when practicing. Play the root with your left hand and sustain it with the damper (sustain) pedal, then lift your hand and play the first rootless voicing (the Phrygian chord) as written. While holding this chord with your left hand, take your foot off the damper (sustain) pedal and play the scale in your right hand. This technique will help you hear the chord from the bottom up, allowing you to get its tonality in your ear. It will also enable you to aurally relate the scale to the chord. (Note: This is for practice only. Do not play and hold the root in an actual playing situation.)

When playing each chord, identify each chord tone in your mind as 9th, 11th, 5th, or root.

After you have gone through this process for all twelve of the Phrygian voicings, repeat the same steps with the second voicing for all twelve of the major triad/major seventh chords. (As we discussed earlier, you can add the major seventh of the triad a half step below the triad to increase the tension.) The second chord is positioned in the second measure for legibility only. You should play this chord the same way that you played the dominant seventh chords, holding down the chord and then playing the entire scale in your right hand up and down two octaves.

Swung Eighth Notes, Articulation and Phrasing

Playing these scales with a swung eighth note feel (as explained in previous volumes of this series) will help you to develop a more authentically "jazz" rhythmic feel.

As you become more comfortable with the actual notes of each scale and chord, you should begin to focus more on the subtleties of articulation. Each scale should be played legato, meaning that the notes are connected. Many jazz piano students make the mistake of trying to play too staccato (disconnected and short), because of the percussive nature of jazz. However, do *not* use the damper or sustain pedal when playing medium tempo or faster jazz eighth note lines. This is another common error made by inexperienced pianists.

The Modes

E Phrygian mode

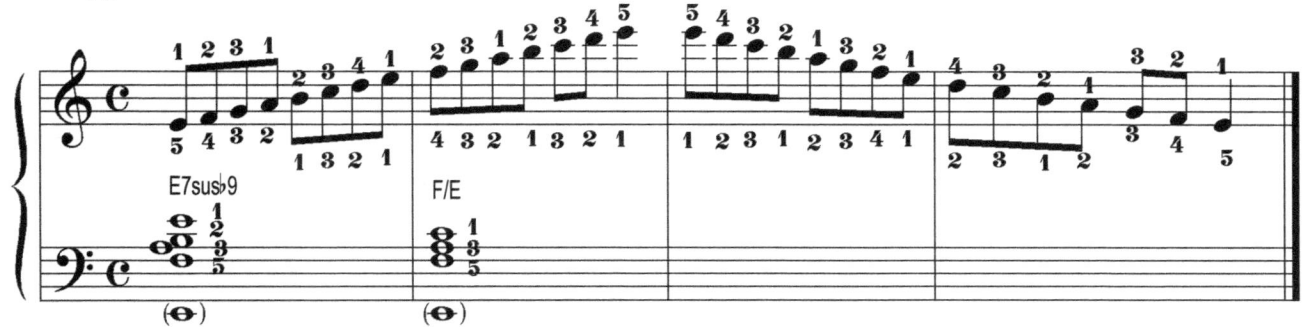

A Phrygian mode

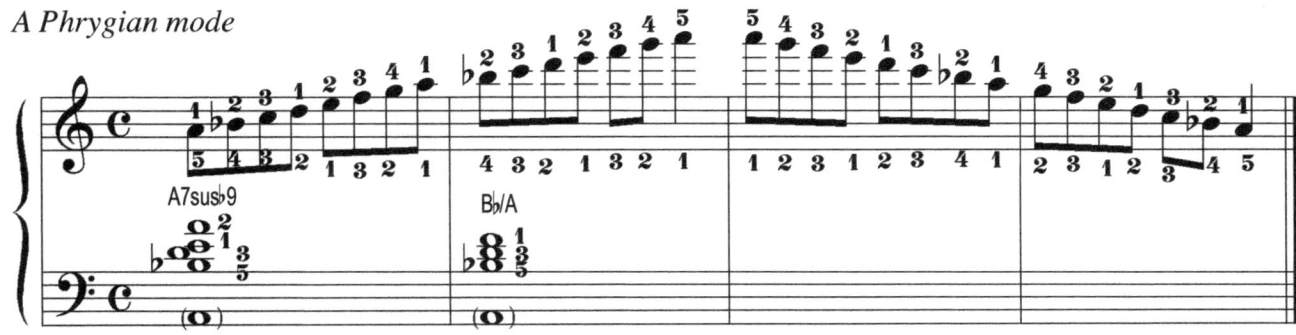

D Phrygian mode

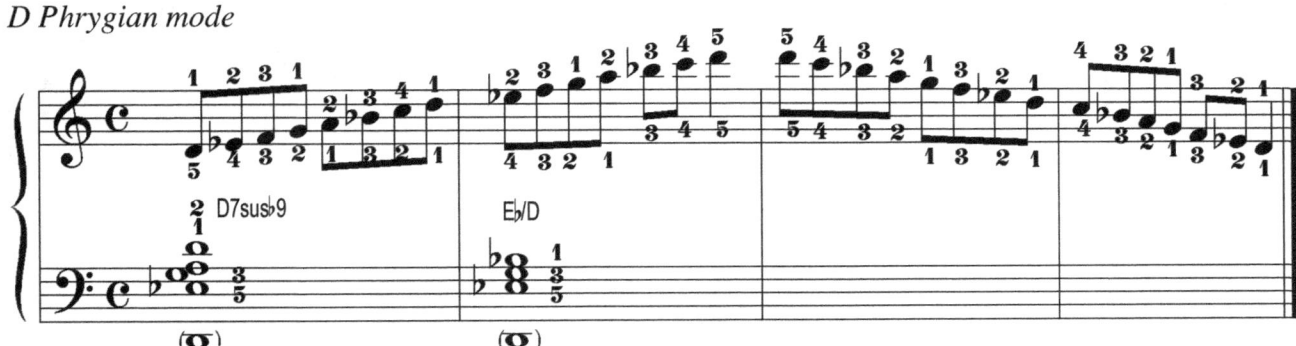

G Phrygian mode

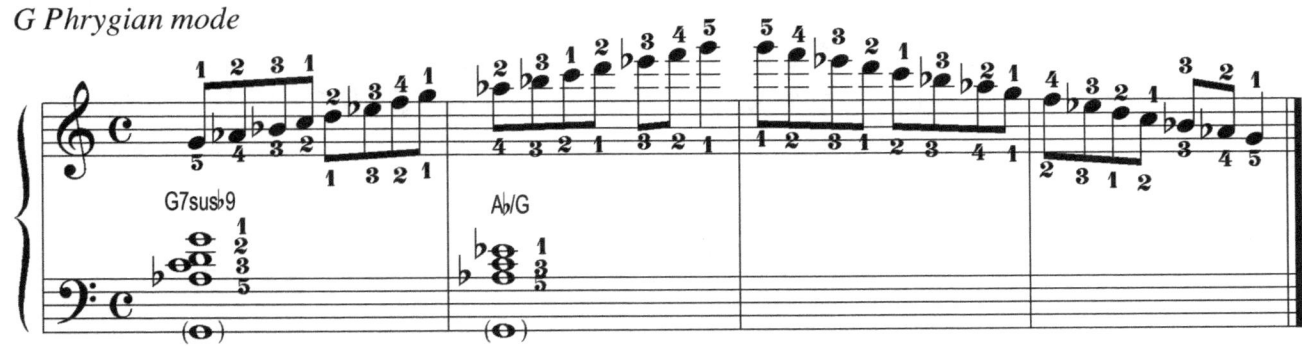

C Phrygian mode

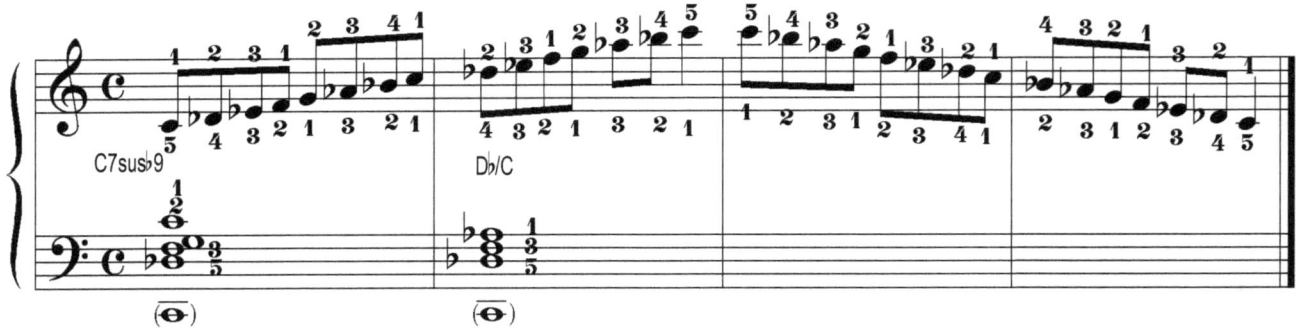

F Phrygian mode

Bb Phrygian mode

D# (Eb) Phrygian mode

G# (Ab) Phrygian

C# (Db) Phrygian mode

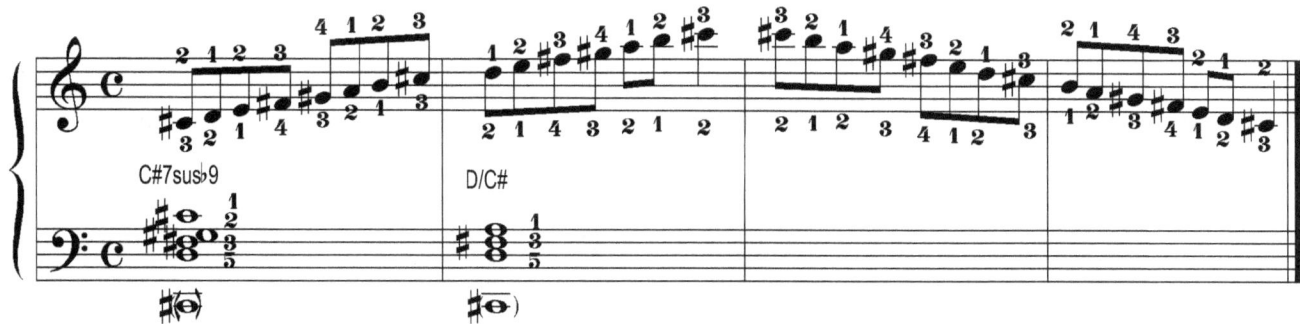

F# (Gb) Phrygian mode

B Phrygian mode

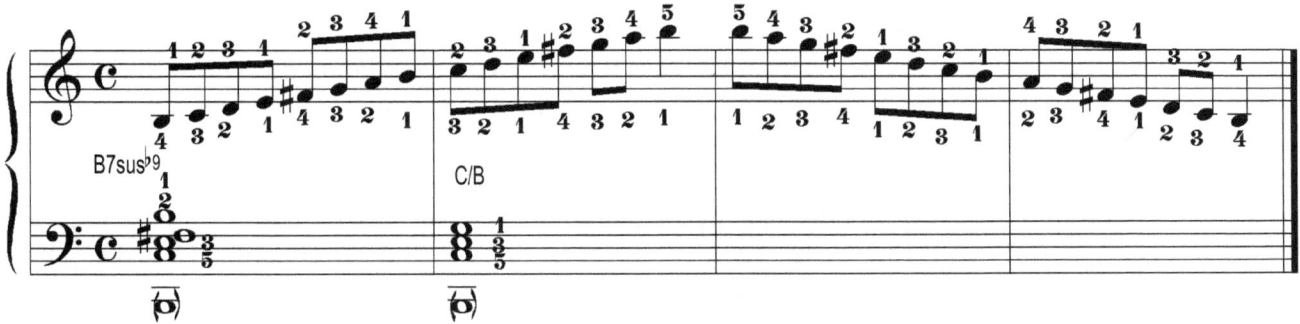

A Modal Approach To Chord Voicings and Comping

So far we have learned only one way to play each chord. There is an approach to left hand voicings that will expand the colors at your disposal. This approach involves taking our chord voicing and moving it up step-wise through the given mode or scale that we are using.

Let us look at an E Phrygian chord with the 11th removed. This gives us an open-sounding voicing consisting of fourths:

We can take each note of this chord and move it up to the next note in the E Phrygian scale, as follows.

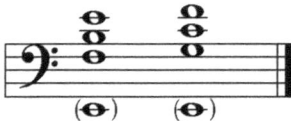

This kind of motion is called stepwise motion, because we are moving up the scale's steps. If we move each of the voices in this chord stepwise through the E Phrygian mode, we derive the following voicings:

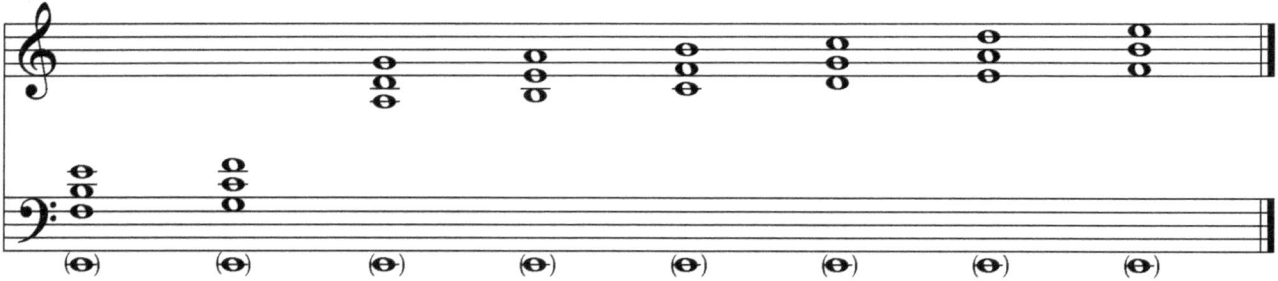

If you play through these voicings you will see that they each work well individually as left-handed Phrygian chord voicings. Perhaps more importantly, they work well together. You can start on any of these voicings and move up and down through them to comp for your right hand. This makes your comping more interesting than if you stay on the same voicing all the time. These types of fourth-based voicings moving through a scale or mode are a signature of the pianist McCoy Tyner.

In the above example, why did we eliminate the 11th from the voicing? This kind of stepwise motion works most consistently with voicings using relatively wide intervals such as fourths. If we keep the eleventh in the voicing, we can still derive some interesting voicings, but several of them will contain more tension and may not be appropriate:

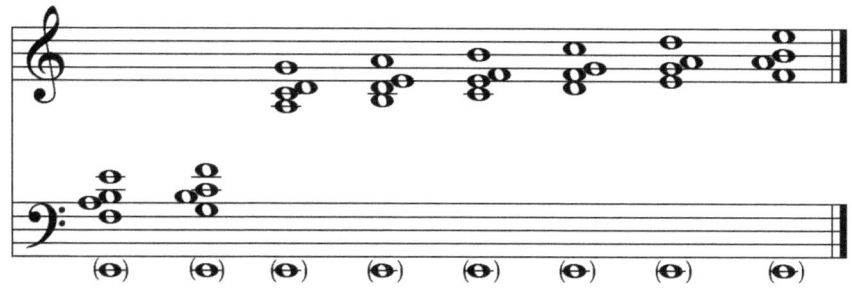

The second voicing in the above progression may sound "wrong" to your ears:

Of course, this is a matter of taste and experience. Furthermore, if you are moving these voicings up and down as you play rather than staying on one particular voicing, you may find the sense of tension and release this creates desirable. Listen to the following example on the Muse-Eek web site under this book's title page:

Example 1

Practice moving both the open 4th voicing and the original Phrygian voicing up and down stepwise though each Phrygian scale. Once you are comfortable doing this your right hand can solo simultaneously.

Suppose you are comping for another instrumentalist such as a saxophonist or trumpeter. Now you have both hands free to comp. Let's expand our E Phrygian voicing in order to use both hands. We can put the 11th (A) up an octave and place the seventh (D) above it. You'll notice that in doing this, we've stacked more fourths on top of our voicing:

Two handed Phrygian chord voicing

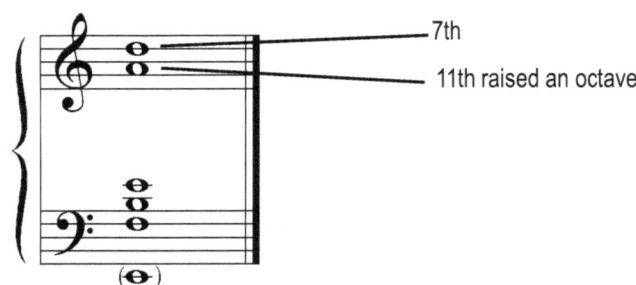

Now we will move this voicing through the Phrygian mode stepwise. (I've placed the bass note on it's own staff for legibility:)

Once again, open fourths work well moving stepwise. Practice this progression on all Phrygian chords, not just E Phrygian.

You can apply this concept to almost any voicing using the scale from which the voicing is derived. As another example, let us take a major triad/major 7th chord. We will move this chord stepwise through the Phrygian mode from which it is derived. Make sure you play the bass note. If there is a bassist you may still want to play the bass note an octave above where it is written to reinforce the sound, because if the bass note can't be heard, it sounds as if you are just playing triads which is not terribly interesting in a jazz context:

Example 2

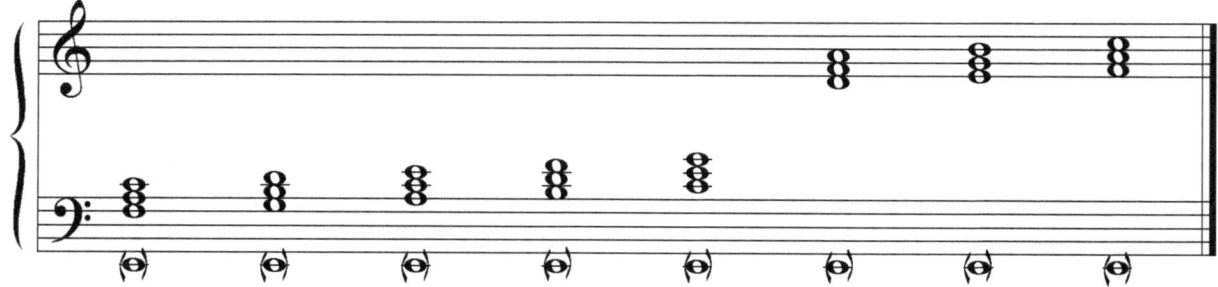

This method of deriving voicings from the scales will work over scales other than the Phrygian. As an exercise, apply this method to other chord/scale combinations with which you are familiar.

Sample Comping Patterns

Below are some comping patterns you can practice which use the Phrygian or Spanish Phrygian scale to derive Phrygian chord voicings. Transpose them into several keys to get used to what they look like and feel like under your fingers. They are all based on the Phrygian chord, but you can apply the rhythmic ideas and the harmonic motion to other chords. These are two-handed patterns, but you can also play just the left hand part while playing lines with your right hand.

Remember that these patterns are merely to help you get started devloping your comping conception. The rhythmic and harmonic decisions you make in your comping will depend on the musical direction of the players, both individually and collectively. Thus, having a set of "stock" comping patterns will not get you as far as having a strong command of the rhythmic and harmonic language of jazz that allows you to comp well in many different situations.

You will notice that some of the examples do not use one particular type of voicing, but mix and match. Having a variety of types of chordal sounds at your disposal will make your comping more interesting and more professional-sounding.

Another way to develop a good rhythmic sense for comping is to listen to and be aware of the snare drum of the drummer. The drummer frequently plays rhythmic patterns on the snare that are similar to those of the comping pianist.

Listening to the great "compers" will help. (See the discography in Volumes 2 or 5 of this series for recommended listening.) These tend to be the players who are most sought out as sidemen or sidewomen because they play appropriately for the musical context and add rhythmic and harmonic interest while also making the soloist feel very comfortable. Some of my favorite compers on the piano include Herbie Hancock, Wynton Kelly, McCoy Tyner, Renee Rosnes, Harold Danko, Ralph Sharon, Gary Fisher, and Jim McNeely.

Example 3

Example 4

Bb Phrygian

Example 5

G Spanish Phrygian

Example 6

Example 7

Example 8

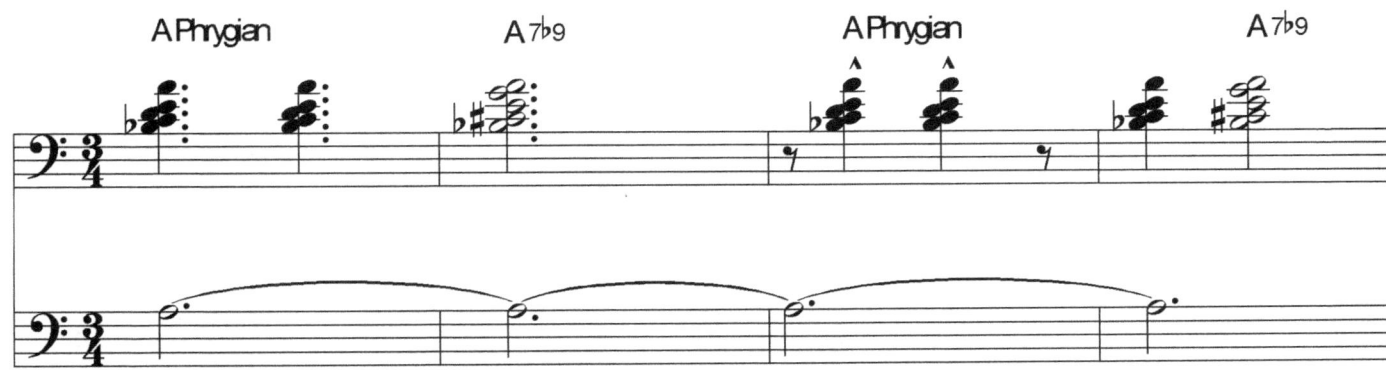

Your Ideas

On the following pages, space is reserved for you to notate voicings you derive from scales you are familiar with, and to work out lines you come up with using the Phrygian mode. Notate which chord you are voicing, and which scale you are deriving the voicings from. It may help you to include fingerings in your notation too.

Two-handed voicings:

chord name:
scale used:

chord name:
scale used:

chord name:
scale used:

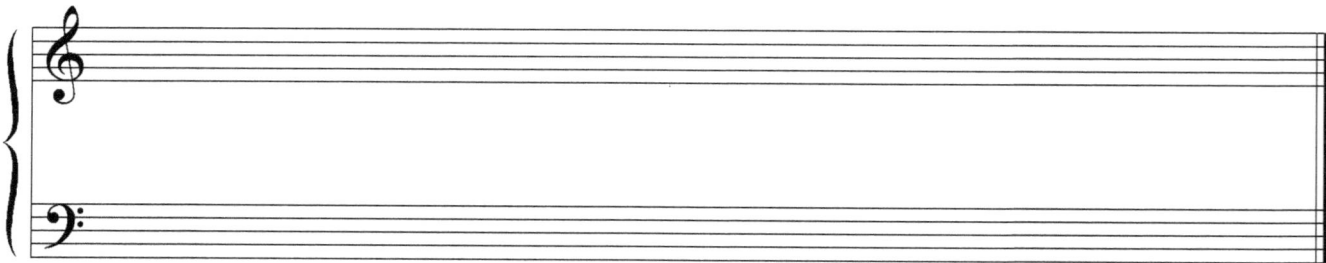

chord name:
scale used:

chord name:
scale used:

chord name:
scale used:

chord name:
scale used:

left-hand voicings:

chord name:
scale used:

chord name:
scale used:

chord name:
scale used:

chord name:
scale used:

chord name:
scale used:

chord name:
scale used:

Phrygian melodic lines:

Phrygian scale used:

Phrygian scale used:

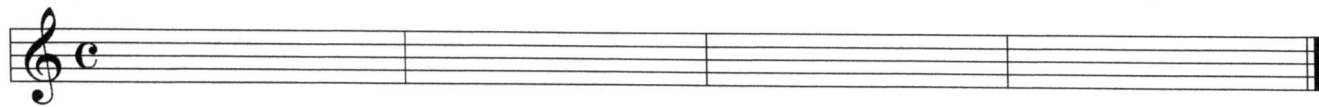

Phrygian scale used:

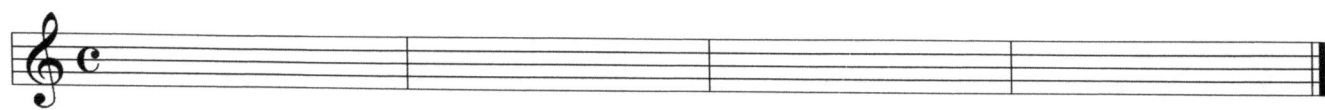

Phrygian scale used:

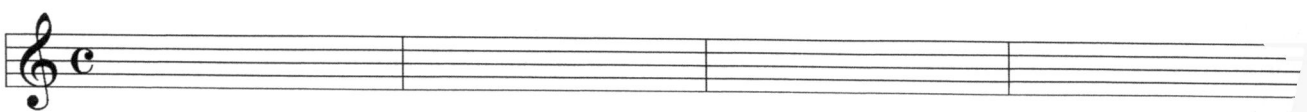

Phrygian scale used:

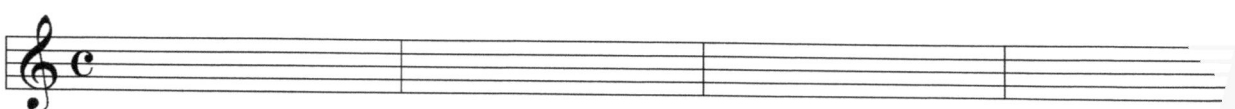

Phrygian scale used:

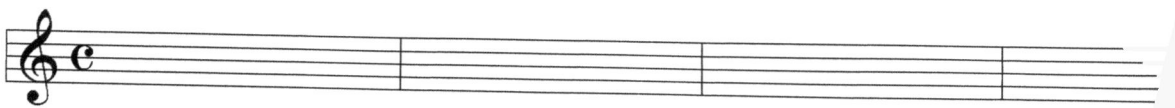

A Phrygian Etude: Apple Flambe (by Virginia Mayhew)

Apple Flambe is a piece written by New York-based saxophonist/arranger/composer Virginia Mayhew. It has been released on her 2004 CD, *No Walls* on Renma Records. As you can see, the piece, with it's sus♭9 chords, is a perfect vehicle for working on Phrygian scales.

Section A of the composition is based on an E♭sus♭9 chord. The melody contains a G♭ which implies the original Phrygian scale as opposed to the Spanish Phrygian.

In Section B, the melody contains both G♭ (the third in the Phrygian scale) and G natural (the third in the Spanish Phrygian scale) over an E♭sus♭9. Section C, which pedals over an Esus♭9 chord, uses both a G and a G# in the melody. Section D uses both an A and a B♭ in the melody over an Fsus♭9. Because the melody in these sections contains both the minor third and the raised third, these chords could imply either a Phrygian or a Spanish Phrygian sound. Therefore, when comping, it is up the pianist's discretion to pay close attention to the melody when deciding which scale to use at any given point.

At the Muse-Eek website, on this book's title page, there is an audio file which illustrates the use of both scales interchangeably over the solo section of this composition. There is also a MIDI file of the solo section that you can play along with. I suggest that you practice the changes in various keys by transposing the chords of the solo section and transposing the MIDI file as well and. At the Muse-Eek website there are links to MIDI players that will allow you to vary the pitch and tempo of the MIDI file so that you can practice along at your own pace.

by playing this tune because each chord change is open to interpretation in terms of the scales u can apply. This gives the piece an open quality that is very exciting to explore as an impro- lso, the tension created through the use of the (already tension-filled) sus♭9 chords ascending ally creates an excitement which is always felt by the musicians and conveyed to the hen this tune is played.

Apple Flambe

Virginia Mayhew

c. 2000 by V. Mayhew

Further Exploration

To get a better sense of how you want to sound as you explore jazz improvisation, it is important to listen to jazz! I have found that many inexperienced players do not have a sense of where to find the right music to listen to.

In Volume 2 of this series, I included an extensive jazz piano discography. In Volume 5, I supplemented this list with some additional jazz piano and keyboard recordings. These two volumes are excellent sources to begin your listening. I also suggest that whenever you get the chance you inquire of artists you admire what they've listened to and what recordings they recommend.

What Next?

If you have mastered the material in this book you are on your way to becoming a versatile jazz pianist. You now have a grasp of some of the "modern" (post-1960) vocabulary of jazz.

One of the activities that will benefit you most as a player is finding other musicians to play with. You will improve more quickly by playing with others. Seek out the best players you can find who are willing to play with you. Don't be afraid to inquire whether people are interested in getting together to play. They can always say no if they are too busy or uninterested.

Another way to help you improve is to record yourself playing occasionally and listen back a day or two later. Do not record yourself every day or you will not be able to hear the improvement and will become frustrated. It is important to be as objective as possible about your playing. Listening to your playing and telling yourself "I stink" will only discourage you. Instead, listen as an outsider: take stock of areas you need to work harder on, as well as noting areas where you have improved.

This book is part of a series of books that focuses on learning and applying jazz scales in order to give you the vocabulary and confidence to become a fluid jazz improvisor. When you are ready, you may wish to build on the progress you've made by choosing another book in this series.

Books Available From
Muse Eek Publishing Company

The Bruce Arnold series of instruction books for guitar are the result of 20 years of teaching. Mr. Arnold, who teaches at New York University and Princeton University has listened to the questions and problems of his students, and written forty books addressing the needs of the beginning to advanced student. Written in a direct, friendly and practical manner, each book is structured in such as way as to enable a student to understand, retain and apply musical information. In short, these books teach.

1st Steps for a Beginning Guitarist
Spiral Bound ISBN 1890944-90-4   Perfect Bound ISBN 1890944-93-9

"1st Steps for a Beginning Guitarist" is a comprehensive method for guitar students who have no prior musical training. Whether you are playing acoustic, electric or twelve-string guitar, this book will give you the information you need, and trouble shoot the various pitfalls that can hinder the self-taught musician. Includes pictures, videos and audio in the form of midifiles and mp3's.

Chord Workbook for Guitar Volume 1 (2nd edition)
Spiral Bound ISBN 0-9648632-1-9   Perfect Bound ISBN 1890944-50-5

A consistent seller, this book addresses the needs of the beginning through intermediate student. The beginning student will learn chords on the guitar, and a section is also included to help learn the basics of music theory. Progressions are provided to help the student apply these chords to common sequences. The more advanced student will find the reharmonization section to be an invaluable resource of harmonic choices. Information is given through musical notation as well as tablature.

Chord Workbook for Guitar Volume 2 (2nd edition)
Spiral Bound ISBN 0-9648632-3-5   Perfect Bound ISBN 1890944-51-3

This book is the Rosetta Stone of pop/jazz chords, and is geared to the intermediate to advanced student. These are the chords that any serious student bent on a musical career must know. Unlike other books which simply give examples of isolated chords, this unique book provides a comprehensive series of progressions and chord combinations which are immediately applicable to both composition and performance.

Music Theory Workbook for Guitar Series

The world's most popular instrument, the guitar, is not taught in our public schools. In addition, it is one of the hardest on which to learn the basics of music. As a result, it is frequently difficult for the serious guitarist to get a firm foundation in theory.

Theory Workbook for Guitar Volume 1
Spiral Bound ISBN 0-9648632-4-3   Perfect Bound ISBN 1890944-52-1

This book provides real hands-on application of intervals and chords. A theory section written in concise and easy to understand language prepares the student for all exercises. Worksheets are given that quiz a student about intervals and chord construction using staff notation and guitar tablature. Answers are supplied in the back of the book enabling a student to work without a teacher.

Theory Workbook for Guitar Volume 2
Spiral Bound ISBN 0-9648632-5-1   Perfect Bound ISBN 1890944-53-X

This book provides real hands-on application for 22 different scale types. A theory section written in concise and easy to understand language prepares the student for all exercises. Worksheets are given that quiz a student about scale construction using staff notation and guitar tablature. Answers are supplied in the back of the book enabling a student to work without a teacher. Audio files are also available on the muse-eek.com website to facilitate practice and improvisation with all the scales presented.

Rhythm Book Series

These books are a breakthrough in music instruction, using the internet as a teaching tool! Audio files of all the exercises are easily downloaded from the internet.

Rhythm Primer
Spiral Bound ISBN 0-890944-03-3   Perfect Bound ISBN 1890944-59-9

This 61 page book concentrates on all basic rhythms using four rhythmic levels. All examples use one pitch, allowing the student to focus completely on time and rhythm. All exercises can be downloaded from the internet to facilitate learning. See http://www.muse-eek.com for details

Rhythms Volume 1
Spiral Bound ISBN 0-9648632-7-8   Perfect Bound ISBN 1890944-55-6

This 120 page book concentrates on eighth note rhythms and is a thesaurus of rhythmic patterns. All examples use one pitch, allowing the student to focus completely on time and rhythm. All exercises can be downloaded from the internet to facilitate learning. See http://www.muse-eek.com for details.

Rhythms Volume 2
Spiral Bound ISBN 0-9648632-8-6   Perfect Bound ISBN 1890944-56-4

This volume concentrates on sixteenth note rhythms, and is a 108 page thesaurus of rhythmic patterns. All examples use one pitch, allowing the student to focus completely on time and rhythm. All exercises can be downloaded from the internet to facilitate learning. See http://www.muse-eek.com for details.

Rhythms Volume 3
Spiral Bound ISBN 0-890944-04-1   Perfect Bound ISBN 1890944-57-2

This volume concentrates on thirty second note rhythms, and is a 102 page thesaurus of rhythmic patterns. All examples use one pitch, allowing the student to focus completely on time and rhythm. All exercises can be downloaded from the internet to facilitate learning. See http://www.muse-eek.com for details.

Odd Meters Volume 1
Spiral Bound ISBN 0-9648632-9-4   Perfect Bound ISBN 1890944-58-0

This book applies both eighth and sixteenth note rhythms to odd meter combinations. All examples use one pitch, allowing the student to focus completely on time and rhythm. Exercises can be downloaded from the internet to facilitate learning. This 100 page book is an essential sight reading tool. See http://www.muse-eek.com for details.

Contemporary Rhythms Volume 1
Spiral Bound ISBN 1-890944-27-0   Perfect Bound ISBN 1890944-84-X

This volume concentrates on eight note rhythms and is a thesaurus of rhythmic patterns. Each exercise uses one pitch which allows the student to focus completely on time and rhythm. Exercises use modern innovations common to twentieth century notation, thereby familiarizing the student with the most sophisticated systems likely to be encountered in the course of a musical career. All exercises can be downloaded from the internet to facilitate learning. See http://www.muse-eek.com for details.

Contemporary Rhythms Volume 2
Spiral Bound ISBN 1-890944-28-9   Perfect Bound ISBN 1890944-85-8

This volume concentrates on sixteenth note rhythms and is a thesaurus of rhythmic patterns. Each exercise uses one pitch which allows the student to focus completely on time and rhythm. Exercise use modern innovations common to twentieth century notation, thereby familiarizing the student with the most sophisticated systems likely to be encountered in the course of a musical career. All exercises can be downloaded from the internet to facilitate learning. See http://www.muse-eek.com for details.

Independence Volume 1
Spiral Bound ISBN 1-890944-00-9   Perfect Bound ISBN 1890944-83-1

This 51 page book is designed for pianists, stick and touchstyle guitarists, percussionists and anyone who wishes to develop the rhythmic independence of their hands. This volume concentrates on quarter, eighth and sixteenth note rhythms and is a thesaurus of rhythmic patterns. The exercises in this book gradually incorporate more and more complex rhythmic patterns making it an excellent tool for both the beginning and the advanced student.

Other Guitar Study Aids

Right Hand Technique for Guitar Volume 1
Spiral Bound ISBN 0-9648632-6-X   Perfect Bound ISBN 1890944-54-8

Here's a breakthrough in music instruction, using the internet as a teaching tool! This book gives a concise method for developing right hand technique on the guitar, one of the most overlooked and under-addressed aspects of learning the instrument. The simplest, most basic movements are used to build fatigue-free technique. Exercises can be downloaded from the internet to facilitate learning. See http://www.muse-eek.com for details.

Single String Studies Volume One
Spiral Bound ISBN 1-890944-01-7   Perfect Bound ISBN 1890944-62-9

This book is an excellent learning tool for both the beginner who has no experience reading music on the guitar, and the advanced student looking to improve their ledger line reading and general knowledge of each string of the guitar. Each exercise concentrates the students attention on one string at a time. This allows a familiarity to form between the written pitch and where it can be found on the guitar along with improving one's "feel" for jumping linearly across the fretboard. Exercises can be downloaded from the internet to facilitate learning. See http://www.muse-eek.com for details.

Single String Studies Volume Two
Spiral Bound ISBN 1-890944-05-X   Perfect Bound ISBN 1890944-64-5

This book is a continuation of Volume One, but using non-diatonic notes. Volume Two helps the intermediate and advanced student improve their ledger line reading and general knowledge of each string of the guitar. Each exercise concentrates the students attention on one string at a time. This allows a familiarity to form between the written pitch and where it can be found on the guitar along with improving one's "feel" for jumping linearly across the fretboard. Exercises can be downloaded from the internet to facilitate learning. See http://www.muse-eek.com for details.

Single String Studies Volume One (Bass Clef)
Spiral Bound ISBN 1-890944-02-5   Perfect Bound ISBN 1890944-63-7

This book is an excellent learning tool for both the beginner who has no experience reading music on the bass guitar, and the advanced student looking to improve their ledger line reading and general knowledge of each string of the bass. Each exercise concentrates a students attention of one string at a time. This allows a familiarity to form between the written pitch and where it can be found on the bass along with improving one's "feel" for jumping linearly across the fretboard. Exercises can be downloaded from the internet to facilitate learning. See http://www.muse-eek.com for details.

Single String Studies Volume Two (Bass Clef)
Spiral Bound ISBN 1-890944-06-8   Perfect Bound ISBN 1890944-65-3

This book is a continuation of Volume One, but using non-diatonic notes. Volume Two helps the intermediate and advanced student improve their ledger line reading and general knowledge of each string of the bass. Each exercise concentrates the students attention on one string at a time. This allows a familiarity to form between the written pitch and where it can be found on the bass along with improving one's "feel" for jumping linearly across the fretboard. Exercises can be downloaded from the internet to facilitate learning. See http://www.muse-eek.com for details.

Guitar Clinic
Spiral Bound ISBN 1-890944-45-9   Perfect Bound ISBN 1890944-86-6

Guitar Clinic" contains techniques and exercises Mr. Arnold uses in the clinics and workshops he teaches around the U.S.. Much of the material in this book is culled from Mr. Arnold's educational series, over thirty books in all. The student wishing to expand on his or her studies will find suggestions within the text as to which of Mr. Arnold's books will best serve their specific needs. Topics covered include: how to read music, sight reading, reading rhythms, music theory, chord and scale construction, modal sequencing, approach notes, reharmonization, bass and chord comping, and hexatonic scales.

The Essentials: Chord Charts, Scales, and Lead Patterns for the Guitar
Saddle Stitched (Stapled) ISBN 1-890944-94-7

This book is truly essential to the aspiring guitarist. It includes the most commonly played chords on the guitar in all keys, plus a bonus of the most commonly used scales and lead patterns. You can quickly learn all the chords, scales and lead patterns you need to know to play your favorite songs-and solo over them, too! "The Essentials" doesn't stop there, though. It also includes chord progressions to help you learn how to chord songs in folk, country, rock, blues and other popular styles. The books contain loads of easy to understand diagrams of chords, scales and lead patterns so you will be up and running in no time!

Sight Singing and Ear Training Series

The world is full of ear training and sight reading books, so why do we need more?
This sight singing and ear training series uses a different method of teaching relative pitch sight singing and ear training. The success of this method has been remarkable. Along with a new method of ear training these books also use CDs and the internet as a teaching tool! Audio files of all the exercises are easily downloaded from the internet at www.muse-eek.com By combining interactive audio files with a new approach to ear training a student's progress is limited only by their willingness to practice!

A Fanatic's Guide to Ear Training and Sight Singing
Spiral Bound ISBN 1-890944-19-X   Perfect Bound ISBN 1890944-75-0

This book and CD present a method for developing good pitch recognition through sight singing. This method differs from the myriad of other sight singing books in that it develops the ability to identify and name all twelve pitches within a key center. Through this method a student gains the ability to identify sound based on it's relationship to a key and not the relationship of one note to another (i.e. interval training as commonly taught in many texts). All note groupings from one to six notes are presented giving the student a thesaurus of basic note combinations which develops sight singing and note recognition to a level unattainable before this Guide's existence.

Key Note Recognition
Spiral Bound ISBN 1-890944-30-3   Perfect Bound ISBN 1890944-77-7

This book and CD present a method for developing the ability to recognize the function of any note against a key. This method is a must for anyone who wishes to sound one note on an instrument or voice and instantly know what key a song is in. Through this method a student gains the ability to identify a sound based on its relationship to a key and not the relationship of one note to another (i.e. interval training as commonly taught in many texts). Key Center Recognition is a definite requirement before proceeding to two note ear training.

LINES Volume One: Sight Reading and Sight Singing Exercises
Spiral Bound ISBN 1-890944-09-2   Perfect Bound ISBN 1890944-76-9

This book can be used for many applications. It is an excellent source for easy half note melodies that a beginner can use to learn how to read music or for sight singing slightly chromatic lines. An intermediate or advanced student will find exercises for multi-voice reading. These exercises can also be used for multi-voice ear training. The book has the added benefit in that all exercises can be heard by downloading the audio files for each example. See http://www.muse-eek.com for details.

Ear Training ONE NOTE: Beginning Level
Spiral Bound ISBN 1-890944-12-2   Perfect Bound ISBN 1890944-66-1

This Book and Audio CD presents a new and exciting method for developing relative pitch ear training. It has been used with great success and is now finally available on CD. There are three levels available depending on the student's ability. This beginning level is recommended for students who have little or no music training.

Ear Training ONE NOTE: Intermediate Level
Spiral Bound ISBN 1-890944-13-0   Perfect Bound ISBN 1890944-67-X

This Audio CD and booklet presents a new and exciting method of developing relative pitch ear training. It has been used with great success and is now finally available on CD. This intermediate level is recommended for students who have had some music training but still find their skills need more development.

Ear Training ONE NOTE: Advanced Level
Spiral Bound ISBN 1-890944-14-9   Perfect Bound ISBN 1890944-68-8

This Audio CD and booklet presents a new and exciting method of developing relative pitch ear training. It has been used with great success and is now finally available on CD. There are three levels available depending on the student's ability. This advanced level is recommended for students who have worked with the intermediate level and now wish to perfect their skills.

Ear Training TWO NOTE: Beginning Level Volume One
Spiral Bound ISBN 1-890944-31-9   Perfect Bound ISBN 1890944-69-6

This Book and Audio CD continues the method of developing relative pitch ear training as set forth in the "Ear Training, One Note" series. There are six volumes in the beginning level series. Through practice, the student eventually gains the ability to recognize the key and the names of any two notes played simultaneously. Volume One concentrates on 5ths. Prerequisite: a strong grasp of the One Note method.

Ear Training TWO NOTE: Beginning Level Volume Two
Spiral Bound ISBN 1-890944-32-7   Perfect Bound ISBN 1890944-70-X

This Book and Audio CD continues the method of developing relative pitch ear training as set forth in the "Ear Training, One Note" series. There are six volumes in the beginning level series. Through practice, the student eventually gains the ability to recognize the key and the names of any two notes played simultaneously. Volume Two concentrates on 3rds. Prerequisite: a strong grasp of the One Note method.

Ear Training TWO NOTE: Beginning Level Volume Three
Spiral Bound ISBN 1-890944-33-5   Perfect Bound ISBN 1890944-71-8

This Book and Audio CD continues the method of developing relative pitch ear training as set forth in the "Ear Training, One Note" series. There are six volumes in the beginning level series. Through practice, the student eventually gains the ability to recognize the key and the names of any two notes played simultaneously. Volume Three concentrates on 6ths. Prerequisite: a strong grasp of the One Note method.

Ear Training TWO NOTE: Beginning Level Volume Four
Spiral Bound ISBN 1-890944-34-3   Perfect Bound ISBN 1890944-72-6

This Book and Audio CD continues the method of developing relative pitch ear training as set forth in the "Ear Training, One Note" series. There are six volumes in the beginning level series. Through practice, the student eventually gains the ability to recognize the key and the names of any two notes played simultaneously. Volume Four concentrates on 4ths. Prerequisite: a strong grasp of the One Note method.

Ear Training TWO NOTE: Beginning Level Volume Five
Spiral Bound ISBN 1-890944-35-1   Perfect Bound ISBN 1890944-73-4

This Book and Audio CD continues the method of developing relative pitch ear training as set forth in the "Ear Training, One Note" series. There are six volumes in the beginning level series. Through practice, the student eventually gains the ability to recognize the key and the names of any two notes played simultaneously. Volume Five concentrates on 2nds. Prerequisite: a strong grasp of the One Note method.

Ear Training TWO NOTE: Beginning Level Volume Six
Spiral Bound ISBN 1-890944-36-X   Perfect Bound ISBN 1890944-74-2

This Book and Audio CD continues the method of developing relative pitch ear training as set forth in the "Ear Training, One Note" series. There are six volumes in the beginning level series. Through practice, the student eventually gains the ability to recognize the key and the names of any two notes played simultaneously. Volume Six concentrates on 7ths. Prerequisite: a strong grasp of the One Note method.

Comping Styles Series

This series is built on the progressions found in Chord Workbook Volume One. Each book covers a specific style of music and presents exercises to help a guitarist, bassist or drummer master that style. Audio CDs are also available so a student can play along with each example and really get "into the groove."

Comping Styles for the Guitar Volume Two FUNK
Spiral Bound ISBN 1-890944-07-6   Perfect Bound ISBN 1890944-60-2

This volume teaches a student how to play guitar or piano in a funk style. 36 Progressions are presented: 12 keys of a Major and Minor Blues plus 12 keys of Rhythm Changes A different groove is presented for each exercise giving the student a wide range of funk rhythms to master. An Audio CD is also included so a student can play along with each example and really get "into the groove." The audio CD contains "trio" versions of each exercise with Guitar, Bass and Drums.

Comping Styles for the Bass Volume Two FUNK
Spiral Bound ISBN 1-890944-08-4   Perfect Bound ISBN 1890944-61-0

This volume teaches a student how to play bass in a funk style. 36 Progressions are presented: 12 keys of a Major and Minor Blues plus 12 keys of Rhythm Changes A different groove is presented for each exercise giving the student a wide range of funk rhythms to master. An Audio CD is also included so a student can play along with each example and really get "into the groove." The audio CD contains "trio" versions of each exercise with Guitar, Bass and Drums.

Jazz and Blues Bass Line
Spiral Bound ISBN 1-890944-15-7   Perfect Bound ISBN 1890944-16-5

This book covers the basics of bass line construction. A theoretical guide to building bass lines is presented along with 36 chord progressions utilizing the twelve keys of a Major and Minor Blues, plus twelve keys of Rhythm Changes. A reharmonization section is also provided which demonstrates how to reharmonize a chord progression on the spot.

Time Series

The Doing Time series presents a method for contacting, developing and relying on your internal time sense: This series is an excellent source for any musician who is serious about developing strong internal sense of time. This is particularly useful in any kind of music where the rhythms and time signatures may be very complex or free, and there is no conductor.

THE BIG METRONOME
Spiral Bound ISBN 1-890944-37-8   Perfect Bound ISBN 1890944-82-3

The Big Metronome is designed to help you develop a better internal sense of time. This is accomplished by requiring you to "feel time" rather than having you rely on the steady click of a metronome. The idea is to slowly wean yourself away from an external device and rely on your internal/natural sense of time. The exercises presented work in conjunction with the three CDs that accompany this book. CD 1 presents the first 13 settings from a traditional metronome 40-66; the second CD contains metronome markings 69-116, and the third CD contains metronome markings 120-208. The first CD gives you a 2 bar count off and a click every measure, the second CD gives you a 2 bar count off and a click every 2 measures, the 3rd CD gives you a 2 bar count off and a click every 4 measures. By presenting all common metronome markings a student can use these 3 CDs as a replacement for a traditional metronome.

Doing Time with the Blues Volume One:
Spiral Bound ISBN 1-890944-17-3   Perfect Bound ISBN 1890944-78-5

The book and CD presents a method for gaining an internal sense of time thereby eliminating dependence on a metronome. The book presents the basic concept for developing good time and also includes exercises that can be practiced with the CD. The CD provides eight 8 minute tracks at different tempos in which the time is delineated every 2 bars, and with an extra hit every 12 bars to outline the blues form. The student may then use the exercises presented in the book to gain control of their execution or improvise to gain control of their ideas using this bare minimum of time delineation.

Doing Time with the Blues Volume Two:
Spiral Bound ISBN 1-890944-18-1   Perfect Bound ISBN 1890944-79-3

This is the 2nd volume of a four volume series which presents a method for developing a musician's internal sense of time, thereby eliminating dependence on a metronome. This 2nd volume presents different exercises which further the development of this time sense. This 2nd volume begins to test even a professional level player's ability. The CD provides eight 8 minute tracks at different tempos in which the time is delineated every 4 bars with an extra hit every 12 bars to outline the blues form. New exercises are also included that can be practiced with the CD. This series is an excellent source for any musician who is serious about developing an internal sense of time.

Doing Time with 32 bars Volume One:
Spiral Bound ISBN 1-890944-22-X   Perfect Bound ISBN Spiral Bound ISBN 1890944-80-7

The book and CD presents a method for gaining an internal sense of time thereby eliminating dependence on a metronome. The book presents the basic concept for developing good time and also includes exercises that can be practiced with the CD. The CD provides eight 8 minute tracks at different tempos in which the time is delineated every 2 bars, with an extra hit every 32 to outline the 32 bar form. The student may then use the exercises presented in the book to gain control of their execution or improvise to gain control of their ideas using this bare minimum of time delineation.

Doing Time with 32 bars Volume Two:
Spiral Bound ISBN 1-890944-23-8   Perfect Bound ISBN Spiral Bound ISBN 1890944-81-5

This is the 2nd volume of a four volume series which presents a method for developing a musician's internal sense of time, thereby eliminating dependence on a metronome.. This 2nd volume presents different exercises which further the development of this time sense. This 2nd volume begins to test even a professional level player's ability. The CD provides eight 8 minute tracks at different tempos in which the time is delineated every 4 bars with an extra hit every 32 bars to outline the 32 bar form. New exercises are also included that can be practiced with the CD. This series is an excellent source for any musician who is serious about developing an internal sense of time.

Other Workbooks

Music Theory Workbook for All Instruments, Volume 1: Interval and Chord Construction
Spiral Bound ISBN 1594899-51-7   Perfect Bound ISBN 1890944-46-7

This book provides real hands-on application of intervals and chords. A theory section written in concise and easy to understand language prepares the student for all exercises. Worksheets are given that quiz a student about intervals and chord construction using staff notation. Answers are supplied in the back of the book enabling a student to work without a teacher.

Jazz Piano Vocabulary by Roberta Piket, Volume 1: The Major Scale
Spiral Bound ISBN 1594899-51-7   Perfect Bound ISBN 1594899-52-5

This book is the 1st volume in a series designed to help the student of jazz piano learn and apply jazz scales by mastering each scale and its uses in improvisation. Each book focuses on a different scale, illustrating the scale in all twelve keys with complete fingerings. Also provided are chords and left hand voicings to match, exercises and etudes to apply the material to improvising, ideas for further study and listening, and detailed suggestions on how to practice the material. Volume 1 also includes a detailed primer on note reading, basic theory and rhythmic notation.

Jazz Piano Vocabulary by Roberta Piket, Volume 2: The Dorian Mode
Spiral Bound ISBN 1890944-96-3   Perfect Bound ISBN 1890944-98-X

The 2nd volume in the series, this book focuses on the Dorian scale and applies it to improvising on minor seventh chords. The Dorian scale is presented in all twelve keys with complete fingerings. The book also contains left hand voicings, exercises, many examples, an etude to help apply the material, ideas for further study, an extended discography, and detailed instructions and practice tips.

Jazz Piano Vocabulary by Roberta Piket, Volume 3: The Phrygian Mode
Spiral Bound ISBN 1594899533   Perfect Bound ISBN 1594899541

For students who have covered the basics in Volumes 1, 2, and 5, this book focuses on the Phrygian and Spanish Phrygian scales. It discusses "modern" jazz chords such as the "Phrygian" chord (sus♭9). The scale is presented in all 12 keys with fingerings. It also provides a detailed treatise on a modal approach to chord voicing, left-hand voicings, practice tips and a Phrygian etude.

Jazz Piano Vocabulary by Roberta Piket, Volume 5: The Mixolydian Mode
Spiral Bound ISBN 1594899576   Perfect Bound ISBN 1594899584

This book focuses on the Mixolydian scale and applies it to improvising on dominant seventh and dominant seventh sus chords. The scale is presented in all twelve keys with fingerings. The book also contains an introduction to approach notes, an explanation and etude on twelve bar blues form, left hand voicings, exercises, melodic examples, instructions and practice tips.

E-Books

The Bruce Arnold series of instructional E-books is for the student who wishes to target specific areas of study that are of particular interest. Many of these books are excerpted from other larger texts. The excerpted source is listed for each book. These books are available on-line at www.muse-eek.com as well as at many e-tailers throughout the internet. These books can also be purchased in the traditional book binding format. (See the ISBN number for proper format)

Chord Velocity: Volume One, Learning to switch between chords quickly
E-book ISBN 1-890944-88-2

The first hurdle a beginning guitarist encounters is difficulty in switching between chords quickly enough to make a chord progression sound like music. This book provides exercises that help a student gradually increase the speed with which they change chords. Special free audio files are also available on the muse-eek.com website to make practice more productive and fun. With a few weeks, remarkable improvement by can be achieved using this method. This book is excerpted from "1st Steps for a Beginning Guitarist Volume One."

Guitar Technique: Volume One, Learning the basics to fast, clean, accurate and fluid performance skills.
E-book ISBN 1-890944-91-2

This book is for both the beginning guitarist or the more experienced guitarist who wishes to improve their technique. All aspects of the physical act of playing the guitar are covered, from how to hold a guitar to the specific way each hand is involved in the playing process. Pictures and videos are provided to help clarify each technique. These pictures and videos are either contained in the book or can be downloaded at www.muse-eek.com This book is excerpted from "1st Steps for a Beginning Guitarist Volume One."

Accompaniment: Volume One, Learning to Play Bass and Chords Simultaneously
E-book ISBN 1-890944-87-4

The techniques found within this book are an excellent resource for creating and understanding how to play bass and chords simultaneously in a jazz or blues style. Special attention is paid to understanding how this technique is created, thereby enabling the student to recreate this style with other pieces of music. This book is excerpted from the book "Guitar Clinic."

Beginning Rhythm Studies: Volume One, Learning the basics of reading rhythm and playing in time.
E-book ISBN 1-890944-89-0

This book covers the basics for anyone wishing to understand or improve their rhythmic abilities. Simple language is used to show the student how to read and play rhythm. Exercises are presented which can accelerate the learning process. Audio examples in the form of midifiles are available on the muse-eek.com website to facilitate learning the correct rhythm in time. This book is excerpted from the book "Rhythm Primer."